T0368089

"MORNING MEDICATIONS";
GOD'S MINUTE PARAPHRASED

CURTIS DAHLGREN

authorHOUSE®

AuthorHouse™
1663 Liberty Drive
Bloomington, IN 47403
www.authorhouse.com
Phone: 833-262-8899

Published by AuthorHouse   12/03/2024

ISBN: 979-8-8230-3353-4 (sc)
ISBN: 979-8-8230-3352-7 (e)

Library of Congress Control Number: 2024919404

Print information available on the last page.

Any people depicted in stock imagery provided by Getty Images are models, and such images are being used for illustrative purposes only. Certain stock imagery © Getty Images.

This book is printed on acid-free paper.

"MORNING MEDICATIONS"; GOD'S MINUTE PARAPHRASED

THAT TITLE is not a typo. A simple morning prayer is still the best medicine. Laughter is second. The daily devotional, God's Minute, has been in my family - and well-used - for probably 100 years. It may be the greatest book of its kind ever published, authored by 360-some pastors who were educated in the 1800s. Their prayers were written like prose or poetry, with a depth of spirituality that would embarrass today's seminaries (er, "cemeteries," where the Truth gets buried).

There may be a Third American Great Awakening ahead, but it won't happen without praying by "those who are called by My Name" (2 Chronicles 7:14).

Dedication
to our Elder Brother and soon-coming King.

Introduction

"You will find that meditation can result in inspiration, aspiration, motivation - even medication!" - Louis O. Caldwell, "Good Morning, Lord; Devotions for College Students," 1971; Baker Books

"God's Minute" is a well-worn devotion book that's been in my family about 100 years. It was written by 360-some pastors who were educated in the 1800s. Their style of poetic prose and depth of spirituality would embarrass some of today's seminaries. I began gleaning nuggets from the day's prayer, condensing them to two lines, and posting them on Facebook as "Morning Medications" (that was before I came across the Caldwell quote), so that's how this little book evolved. Your mission, should you choose to accept it, is to go and likewise share your favorites.

If you contacted nine people, and they contacted nine different people, and this continued for just ten days, you could reach half the population of the world, President Reagan used to say. America's First Great Awakening was in the 1700s and it prepared the way for our Independence; the 2nd one in yhe 1800s saved the Union and freed the slaves. I hope to live to see the start of a Third Great Awakening to save America and/or "prepare the way of the Lord." Part 1 tells why we need such an Awakening.

PART 1

It Is Time, Lord, For You To Work

"The wicked plots against the just and gnashes against him with his teeth. The Lord shall laugh at the wicked for He sees that His day is coming. The wicked have drawn out the sword, and have bent their bow, to slay those who are upright of conversation. Their sword shall enter into their own heart, and their bows shall be broken." - Psalm 37:12-15

For then shall be great tribulation, such as was not since the beginning of the world to that time, no, nor ever shall be; and except those days be shortened, there would be no flesh saved, but for the elect's sake those days WILL be shortened." - Matthew 24:21-22

It is time, Lord, for you to work, for they have made void thy Law." - Psalm 119:126

Though the number of the children of Israel be as the sands of the sea a remnant will be saved, for He will finish the work, and cut it short in righteousness, because a SHORT WORK will the Lord work upon the earth." Romans 9:27-28

Wonder marvelously, for I will work a work in your day that you will not believe, though it be told to you." - Habakkuk 1:5

Verily, verily, I say unto you, he who believes on Me, the works that I do he will do also, and greater works than these shall he do, because I go to My Father." - John 14:12

O Lord revive your work in the midst of the years, in the midst of the the years make known. In wrath remember mercy. - Habakkuk 3:2

This gospel of the kingdom shall be diseminated to the whole world for a witness unto all nations. - Matthew 24:14

The stouthearted have slept their sleep, but at Thy rebuke You caused judgment to be heard from heaven; the earth feared and was still. - Psalm 76:5,8-10

While the bridegroom tarried, they all slumbered and slept, and at midnight there was a cry made, Behold the bridegroom is coming, and all the virgins woke up. -Matthew 25:5-7

God pours contempt upon princes and causes them to wander in the wilderness . .The righteous shall see it and rejoice and all iniquity shall stop her mouth. -Psalm 107:40-42

He makes wars to cease unto the ends of the earth - He breaks the bow and cuts the spear in two He burns the chariot in the fire. Be still and know that I am God. - Psalm 46:9-10

Alas for that day is great so that there is none like it - It is the time of Jacob's trouble BUT he will be saved out of it. For I am with thee saith the Lord to save thee though I make a full end of the nations- I will correct you in measure. - Jeremiah 30:7- 11

The nations shall see and be confounded . . They shall lay their hands upon their mouths - they shall be afraid of our God and shall fear because of thee - Who is a God like YOU who passes over the transgression of the remnant of His heritage and delights in compassion — Thou wilt perform the truth to JACOB and the mercy to Abraham which was sworn unto our fathers from the days of old. - Micah7:16-20:

The kings of the earth set themselves and the rulers take counsel together against the Lord and His annointed . . He Who sits in the heavens shall laugh; the Lord shall have them in derision. Then He shall speak unto them in His wrath. . . Be wise now therefore, o ye kings. - Psalm 2:2-5,10

Rend your hearts and not your garments; who knows if He will return and repent of the evil? - Joel 2:14

O Lord God of Israel, awake to visit the heathen . . . They belch out with their mouth; swords are in their lips, for who say they, hears, but You, O Lord will laugh at them; You will have all the heathen in derision. -Psalm 59:5, 7

The wicked plot against the just, and gnash against him with his teeth, The Lord shall laugh at him, for He sees that His day is coming. - Psalm 37::12-13

How long, Eternal? - David

How long go ye limping between two opinions? - Elijah

How long you simple ones, will you love stupidity and the scorners delight in their scorning? And fools hate knowledge? Turn at My reproof - behold I will pour out My Spirit unto you. . I will also laugh at your calamity and I will mock when your fear comes [if you don't turn]. - Proverbs 1:22, 26

The righteous also shall see, and fear, and laugh at him, for this is the man who made not God his strength. - Psalm 52:6-7

The wicked shall see and be grieved. - Psalm 112:10

Blessed are you who weep now, for you shall laugh. - Luke 6:21

[Comment]

GOD'S LAUGH IS NOT A "NANA NANA NA NA LAUGH; IT'S MORE LIKE SARAH'S LAUGH - "God has made me to laugh so that all who hear will laugh with me . .

Who would have said to Abraham, Sarah will give birth in old age." - Genesis 21:6-7

There was one work people wouldn't have believed even if it had been told them, the birth of Isaac. Isaac means "HE WILL LAUGH" (#3446 in Strong's concordance).

HE INHERITED HIS MOTHER'S SENSE OF HUMOR. Sarah's laugh wasn't a sin. Sarah's first thought may have been that having a baby was impossible, but even if it happened it would be funny would be funny (what would people think?).

Back to the present: Go thy way Daniel, for the words are sealed until the time of the end - none of the wicked shall understand, but the wise shall understand. - Daniel 12:9-10

CONCLUSION: IF WE UNDERSTAND MOST OF THE BOOK OF DANIEL, WE MUST BE CLOSE TO THE TIME OF THE END (a time of division and Great Hatred)

The days of visitation are come - the days of recompence are come. Israel shall know it. The prophet is a fool and the spiritual man is "mad," for the multitude of your iniquity and THE GREAT HATRED. - Hosea 9:7

For the vision is yet for an appointed time, but at the end it shall speak and not lie - though it tarry, wait for it. Write the vision that he may run who reads it - Habakkuk 2 -2:3

So shall He "sprinkle" many nations; the kings shall shut their mouths at him, for that which they had not been told they shall see, and that which they had not HEARD they shall consider. - Isaiah 52-15

And it shall come to pass in the last days saith God, I will pour out my Spirit upon ALL flesh, and your sons and your daughters shall prophecy; Your young men shall see visions and your old men shall dream dreams, and on my servants and on my handmaidens I will pour out in those days my Spirit. - Acts 2:17-

When the day of Pentecost was fully come . . . they were all amazed - because they "heard" the Galileans speak every man in his own tongue - dwellers in Mesopotamia, in Egypt, in parts of Libya - Arabians - "we HEAR them speak in our tongues the wonderful works of God." - Acts 2:1-11

NOW LEARN A PARABLE OF THE FIG TREE - WHEN HIS "BRANCH" - twig or bud - IS YET TENDER, YOU KNOW THAT SUMMER IS NIGH - SO LIKEWISE WHEN YOU SHALL SEE ALL THESE THINGS,

KNOW THAT IT IS NEAR - EVEN AT THE DOORS. - Matthew 24:32-33

Behold I will send you Elijah the prophet before the coming of the great and dreadful Day of the Lord lest I come and smite the earth with a curse. - Malachi 4:5-6

I will send My messenger and he will prepare the way before Me, and I will be a swift witness against those who fear Me not . . Then those who feared the Lord SPOKE OFTEN ONE TO ANOTHER . . [THINK TELEGRAPH, TELEPHONE, CELL PHONES, TEXTING, E-MAIL, TWEETING, ETC!]. . and the Lord heard it and a book of remembrance was written before Him for [or OF them (Oxford Bible) or BY them?] those who feared Him and thought upon His name, and they shall be mine saith the Lord in that day when I make up MY JEWELS. - Malachi 3: 1, 5, 16-17

P.S - The theme of this study is WORK - as in "My Father works and I work." - John 5:17

Behold you despisers and wonder - for I will work in your days, a work which you shall in no way believe though a man declare it unto you. - Acts 13:41

STRONG'S #2040 (from 2041

noun = toil, act, deedm effort

adverb - (2040) "I will toil in your days" fig., "TEACH" - from Habakkuk 1:5

to do or make, to practice, ordain, "wrought" - as in "What hath God wrought?" (the Bell telephone, for example} #6466 & 646

PPS: One time I gave this study as a presentation and at the end a guy asked, "But what will the work be?" And I said:

"I don't have to tell you that, because you wouldn't believe it even if I told you."

There are many surprises in store for you, even if you are a believer. Praise the Lord; the Lord provides!

01-01 We commend our family, friends, brethren, and this fair land to Thy fatherly care, Father. May this year not be the worst of times. Let Thy Kingdom come, Lord. Amen!

01-02 Today we pray for snow plow drivers, police officers, and first rsponders, and the people on the highways, Father. Hasten the day of the Proclamation of the Acceptable Year.

01-03 We who subsist under the cover of Your patience now say, give us this day our daily bread, as well as the nourishment we need for our spiritual existence, Father. Selah.

01-04 As our Elder Brother and High Priest hath taught us to call Thee "Father," we come to Thee to ask what Thou art bidding us to do this day. Work with us so we can work with Thee.

01-05 O Lord Our Father, through Your Son and His Word, lead us to higher levels of thought and purpose. Especially bless we pray those who bless You, but bless the whole human race.

01-06 We approach Thee in the name of our Redeemer to render thanksgiving for Thy mercies as we deal with the weather and other trials in life, Father. Make us channels of blessings.

01-07 We know, Father, that only a nation on its knees can stand before its enemies. Have mercy, and incline the hearts of those who know Thee not to come running unto Thee. Amen.

01-08 Thank You for a strong staff to lean on in our upward journey, Father. For Your Son's sake, let all men see that we have been walking with Thee. Help us to truly follow Him.

01-09 Our Father, we gather at Thy feet, Judge of the Supreme Court of heaven, through our Elder Brother, All-in-all, and Friend. Set us upon the path upon which Your blessings can fall.

01-10 We praise with glad hearts the revealed infinity and eternity of Your goodness and power, Father. Help us to love the privilege of prayer and service, in His name, amen.

01-11 When Thou dost call us Home, whether it be in the morning, mid-day, or the sunset of old age, help us to be ready, Father, with our lamps brightly burning we pray. Thank You.

01-12 We seek first today the grace for motives for humble as well as high deeds, Father, so that You might not only dwell in us, but work through us to help prepare for the Coming.

01-13 Thank You for the Words of Your Son who said "Let not your hearts be troubled," Father. Let those words be written on our hearts as well as our minds. And "let there be an answer."

01-14 We give thanks to Thee for the night's sweet rest, Father. Help us to use the rest of the day usefully, for the sake of Your Son, our Redeemer, and for His coming Kingdom. Amen.

01-15 The call to prayer comes at any hour, Lord, but especially when Thou hast kindled the dawn as if the day were made just for us. Hear us and let Your power be great in the earth.

01-16 As children of our heavenly Father, we thank You for our gifts, and for the privilege of being liberal with them - money, talents, and time. Thy will be done. Forgive shortcomings.

01-17 Give us strength this morning Father, and the grace to walk in a clearer light. Comfort those who mourn the loss of someone who was dear to them. Help those who need help.

01-18 May we as a family realize this day, "The path of the just is like a light that shines more and more unto the perfect day," Father. We seek Your benediction this morning. Praise be!

01-19 Suffer us not, we beseech Thee, to become the prey of useless forebodings, nor to lose the things that belong to our peace. Keep our faces to the light and shadows behind us.

01-20 Bless us as individuals too, Father, but we bring to Thee our spiritual family. If any are sick, troubled, or tempted, be unto them the Great Physician. Thank You in the Son's name.

01-21 We come before You as children to a loving Father. Bless the church and our nation that the high hopes of people in distress may not be shattered. Fit us for the duties of the day.

01-22 Forgive our stumbling, Father, and save us from the flattery of all forms of godlessness. Help us to focus on whatsoever things are beautiful, true, and virtuous, and of good repute.

01-23 Abba Father, one day closer to the Kingdom of God on earth, we place our hands in Thine that we may be led in a way that may glorify Thee and make our lives more fruitful.

01-24 Our heavenly Father, we thank Thee that hour by hour our lives are enriched by the knowledge of Him Who revealed Thyself to us. Hear us on behalf of our loved ones. Amen.

01-25 Holy heavenly Father, You have sheltered this family, bearing our burdens and supplying our needs. Bless those who are making known the Gospel of the Kingdom. PTL.

01-26 Father Father, our heavenly Father, we bring ourselves to You as a thank offering this morning.

Quicken us so that we may seek first Your Kingdom and Your righteousness today.

01-27 Teach us to pray, Father, that we may learn the power of purity and trust. Let us fear no evil, not evil men, nor any virus, nor any other illnesses. Hear us and heal us. Allelulia.

01-28 Send forth Your quickening spirit Lord, that we this day may be inspired to higher and nobler thoughts through the power of Your holy spirit in us, that we may redeem the time.

01-29 Give us this day our daly food and fire in the belly, for as our Father and Creator You have claims upon us. Help us to purchase our opportunities and to use our Freedom. Amen!

01-30 May this family and Your chuch on earth seek our daily redemption, sustenance, guidance, and protection, Father. Inspire, direct, encourage, and save us, Lord Yahweh.

01-31 O God of Abraham, Isaac, and Israel, thank You for the mercy seat to which we can come, through the veil opened for us by Your Son. Walk with us as to Emmaus today. Selah.

02-01 While we lay wrapped in slumber, Your sleepless eyes have brought us to the light of a new morning, Lord. Aid us in our efforts to avoid the mistakes of yesterday and yesteryear.

02-02 Father Father, may every day bring us a more perfect trust in Thee, so that in the days of our lives we may become more like Him who taught us to pray "Our Father . . ." Amen.

02-03 Thank You, thank You Father, for food and raiment, plus the Armor of God, as we live to wrestle one more day against wicked spirits in high places, with the sword of Thy good spirit.

02-04 Finally, may we be strong in the Lord and in the power of His might against rulers of Darkness. Quicken us in this quiet hour to stand still and see the salvation of Israel's God.

02-05 Thank You Father for Your kindness. You do provide and we have been given another day. As the world groans, we pray for those who still do not have eyes to see. Praise be.

02-06 As Peter said, "to all who believe," You are precious Father, to whom we go without ceasing. Widen our horizons as we seek first of all the Kingdom to come, soon. Halleluia.

02-07 Help us o Lord to come a little nearer to the Christ example, that we may bespeak His character to those we come in contact with today, and make the Gospel speak clearly. PTL.

02-08 May our hands and heads work for Thee. May our hearts beat for Thee. And may we be healthy enough to serve Thee, Father. Help us to help those who need help today. Amen.

02-09 Father we thank you for home, family, friends, and brethren. Set Your angels about us, and set our minds on Thee and on things above, plus the Work at hand this morning. Selah.

02-10 Father of our Lord and Redeemer, of Whom the whole family in heaven and earth is named, keep us in Thy faith and fear. We offer Thee our thoughts, words, and deeds.

02-11 We thank You that with care You have brought us into another day with its unique obligations and requirements, Father. Bless the police and first responders. Amen.

02-12 As Your servant Abraham Lincoln said, thank You for some of the richest soil on earth, and our salubrious climate. We are indeed privileged to work for the Divine Husbandman.

02-13 Thou dost neither slumber nor sleep, and Your protecting hand has been beneath us and about us, setting a new day before us, so help us make good use of it, Father. Halleluia.

02-14 In the strength of Your name we go forth to meet the duties of the day. As the day, let our strength be. If possible, help us bear some of the burdens of others, Father. Praise be.

02-15 In Your holy presence, in the name of Your Son, we bow today as a household. May it ever be a household of faith. Give us grace and guidance to live up to the Faith of our fathers.

02-16 Heavenly Father, clease us of the tendency to sin by thought, word, deed, and/or omission. Our words are too poor to express our gratitude, but we marvel at Thy mercy. PTL.

02-17 Thank You for the doorway of a new day, Father. May Your Philadelphian church take advantage of the open door before it, and help prepare the way for Thy coming, asap, amen.

02-18 May it be Thy good pleasure to behold this family circle meditating on things above. And may we in due time be joined to that great family circle of kin who have gone on before.

02-19 We lift up our eyes unto the hills, the heavenly hills, from whence cometh our help. As Moses on the mountaintop, let us be closer to You than ever before, one day at a time. PTL.

02-20 As children of our heavenly Father, we look up and know You are waiting on us every morning and Your everlasting arms enfold us. Let Your spirit in us become obvious to others.

02-21 Let us draw nigh unto You, God of Abraham. May we see things in a heavenly light, that we may have hearts that are informed and minds that can know the meaning of Your Love.

02-22 Most generous Father, thank You for the 13 colonies whose spirit produced 50 states dedicated to the proposition that where the Spirit of the Lord is *there* is Liberty. Save us.

02-23 May we have the Faith that hopes all things, Father. And we certainly are like children to You; we have their weaknesses, but without their humility or unwavering trust, so help us.

02-24 Father, God, we thank You this morning for the privilege of living. We count time by breaths and heart beats. Help us show our appreciation by our work. How long, Eternal?

02-25 The way is long and sometimes weary, Father. Start us forth each day with fresh courage, we pray. May the lightest of our burdens be our consciences, thank You. Selah.

02-26 Early, satisfy us with Your mercy, and let the beauty of the Lord be upon us, the work of Your hands. At this point in time we look for the glorious appearing of the King of Kings.

02-27 How precious is the privilege of knowing that we are in the circle of Your care, Father. Whatever this day brings, may Your grace be sufficient for us Your grateful children. Amen.

02-28 Father, You said "As many as I love, I chasten." Thou, Thyself, art more than all Your gifts, so help us to heed Your chastenings, and open the door when you knock. Thank You.

02-29 Thank You for today, Father. You only know what our tomorrows hold for us, so fill our hearts with love that in the depths of our souls we may be grateful for Thine extra blessings.

03-01 Almighty fatherly God, You know what we need better than we do, but above all let us be bent on seeking godliness and the Kingdom of God today and all days, one at a time. PTL.

03-02 Thank You for the day that is before us, another of many blessings, Father. Help us to go out renewed in body and spirit, to the end that we may show our gratitude indeed. Amen.

03-03 Now rested, we pray for preparation for whatever You have planned for us today, and may we become more worthy of larger service, Father, more like the Messiah each day.

03-04 Thank You Father for the mercies of the night, for daily opportunity for usefulness, and spirits capable of living with You everlastingly. Forbid that we should sin by forgetting prayer.

03-05 Father in heaven, thank You for work and the rest during the night; for food, shelter, and clothing; for vocations to which You have called us, and for the coming Kingdom! Selah.

03-06 Eternal Father! Before we go out to our tasks, we come and seek and ask for the fortification of our spirits. Let no evil blight this day, and bring us home safely tonight. Amen.

03-07 Forgive us the sins past and send us forth to our tasks with a song in our hearts, Father. You neither slumber nor sleep, so when our work is done and the night comes, be with us.

03-08 Forgive and forget our past failings, Father, and send us forth with the spirit of power and sound minds. Help us to do what we can to hasten the coming of Your Kingdom, PTL.

03-09 Father Father, our hope of redemption, we tried the world's ways and came back empty, to be filled with Your spirit and Word. Bring us by and by to our Brother's Kingdom.

03-10 You know what our weaknesses are, Father, but we come as more than conquerers through the power and love of Your Son our Saviour. Help us to make the world happier.

03-11 We come to Thee with the confidence and trust of children to their Father. Prosper and protect Your church in all lands, and as we grow in years, may we grow in grace. Hallelu.

03-12 We come to Thee at the start of the day for Your blessing. Let Your everlasting arms be beneath us as we go out into the world to do what You would have us do today. Selah.

03-13 Our heavenly Father and our God, give grace unto this humble family circle. Thank you for Thy gifts day by day. Help our nation and Your church to be a channel of blessing. AMEN.

03-14 Thank You for these hours of sleep, Father. Now let us offer our lives to You. Use each of us as You see fit. Let Your Kingdom come to the ends of the earth as soon as possible. PTL.

03-15 Father, we turn a page again this morn and lay our hands in Thine. As we go out to new tasks, set Your angels about us and lead us in the right direction. Hallowed be Thy name.

03-16 As You so loved the world that You gave Your Son, and He gave Himself, we are in awe of both Your power and Your love. Thank You also for the sacrifices of our earthly parents.

03-17 O Lord our Lord, our fathers' God, let Thy names be exalted in all the earth. Let your Spirit be outpoured upon it and these sorrow filled days be ended. Glory halleluia!

03-18 Father, we enter upon the duties of this day with our hands and hearts joined. Let the Spirit that tugs at our hearts enable us to have clearly dedicated hands, minds, and wills.

03-19 We commend ourselves to Thee, along with our land of Liberty, that lawlessness may be ended and true religion exalted in grace, gifts, and godliness. Selah.

03-20 Though our wicked foes would sow doubt and distrust, Father, we Your children know You better than they, so who can be against us? Let them keep silent. AMEN.

03-21 Encompass with Thy power, Father, Your pastors, prophets, and witnesses, as the laity goes about our daily work. Lift our eyes beyond our local horizons to times immemorial. PTL.

03-22 Gracious Father, we accept the privilege of entering into Thy holy presence through Your Son, our Advocate, as we become conscious of our shortcomings. Praise Thee.

03-23 Father, help us to so live this day that people will see that we carry the Spirit of the Master with us, that they may be prompted to seek Him too. Verily, verily!

03-24 We seek wise thoughts this morning, Father. Help us to see things as they are. And also as they ought to be in a world reconciled to Thee through Jesus, Jeshua, Your Son. Selah.

03-25 Let the power of our Lord be great today. Cast doubts into the sea and move mountains of obstacles out of our way, as we accompany Thee, as a man talks with a friend. Praise be!

03-26 Thank You for life and the morning light, Father. Lighten the darkness of those who doubt. Help us reflect Your light in a fallen world. Lighten the burdens of our people. Amen.

03-27 May we give thanks for blessings day to day, seen and unseen, under Your care. Father. May You write over every door sill, "Peace be unto this household." Thanks again. Let it be.

03-28 Thank You for the common mercies and gifts that we are not taking for granted, Father. Grant the unchurched a vision of their needs, a dream of hope, and better lives. Selah.

03-29 SHELTERED as we are in Your family, we pray for wandering souls, that they have a better mind and may be turned back toward their Father's House. AMEN.

03-30 We need You in the daylight as well as at midnight, so we come to our heavenly Father for directions for the day. We need Your "nurture and admonition" today. Sincerely, us.

03-31 We bow before You with confidence through Christ, Father, thankful for blessings uncountable. Reveal Yourself to the ungrateful. In wrath remember mercy. Halleluia.

04-01 Help us to pray we pray, Father. Shed abroad Your love in our hearts that we might be a blessing to all with whom we come in contact. Through Christ our Saviour. AH-men.

04-02 Father, we love this moment at the commencement of another day as we look up to commune with You. Let our lights so shine that others may come to seek You too. Selah.

04-03 Help us every day, Father, to bear witness and stand fast in the Faith for the Faith.

04-04 Infinite Father, in Whom we live and move and have our being, we begin the day glad to be alive, and ask: help us get the utmost out of the day in the sense of service to others.

04-05 Thank You for the restful curtains of the night, and for the laughter of little children who don't know the difference between the left and the right yet. Be unto us our Father too.

04-06 Father Father, our heavenly Father, continue to make Thyself manifest, and help us to see the larger meaning of little things, "evidence of things not seen." Thy Kingdom come.

04-07 Father, renew a right spirit within us, and fill our hearts with a deeper love for You, Your Son, and our neighbor. Perhaps we can win some soul for You soon. Hallelu.

04-08 May You come unto us "as the rain, as the latter and former rain upon the earth," Father. Let not liberty of thought sully the simple Faith of our Fathers. Praise ye the Lord.

04-09 We appeal this morning for guidance as we face the duties and privileges of the day, Father. Cause Your Spirit to dwell in us richly, and cause Your Kingdom to come, ASAP, pls.

04-10 Father, bring us to the end of this day stronger, wiser, and more able to serve You.

04-11 May this be a glad undefiled day, Father. We are anxious only about doing Your will.

04-12 May we bow before You this morning, Father. Bow Your ear and pour out Your spirit upon the earth as soon as possible.

04-13 [evening prayer] Into Thy hands, Father, we commend our bodies, minds, and our whole essence, that we may have such sleep as will fit us for our duties tomorrow. PTL.

04-14 We come in His name, Your Son's, asking comfort for the grieving, favor for the afflicted, and for the completion of the work of disseminating the Gospel. Selah.

04-15 May the witnessing of Believers, even in hostile lands, make Your plan of salvation known in all lands,

Father, and give special courage to those in dangerous places. Amen.

04-16 We Thy children invoke Your blessing this day, Father. Prompt us to do what we can for others, and gird us with courage to oppose evil men whenever we should. Hallelulia !!

04-17 Father, no ruler on earth is as open to his subjects as You are, so - emboldened by Your promises - we come to Thee again. Help us to have a nice day. And You too. Yes, let it be.

04-18 May our gratitude show, and let our witnessing be effective by deeds if not words. Work in Your children unstained by sin, restraining the wicked spirits in the schools.

04-19 May Christ the redeemer so dwell in our hearts that You, Father, may rule and over-rule our puny wills. And let godliness begin to prevail in county, state, and country. Amen!

04-20 Lord over heaven and earth, Who sets the boundaries of the sea, bless our going out and our coming in like the tides. And help us to batten the hatches if storms should arise.

04-21 How shall we know the deep joys of the soul unless Your Spirit resides in us, Father? How shall we overcome and endure to the end without the help of the Most High God?

04-22 Thank You for many blessings and privileges, Father. Give us the hand of help for any whose needs have claims upon us and may our religion be appetizing to others. Selah.

04-23 Who knows what a day may bring, but we entrust ourselves to the One Who never slumbers. If tempted, we trust Your still small voice, and the silent voice, Your Word. PTL.

04-24 HOLY FATHER, thank You for the gifts of life, love, and laughter. Thank you for a reason to live and the ability to reason. We pray for rectitude in our reasoning with actions to follow.

04-25 OUR FATHER! We are little children yet in Your sight, which is not a bad thing to be. Grant to all of Your children the filial heart, teachable heads, and hands that are clean.

04-26 *WISE* Father, we tend to be short-sighted, so expand our horizons day over day. Guide us safely, through Him Who loves us. If any trouble awaits us, help us to handle it okay.

04-27 May we not be stuck in the present horizons, but looking forward to the coming of the Kingdom, Father.

04-28 "Pray without ceasing, quench not the Spirit," Paul said, so let us draw nearer to You each day because You first drew us to the compehension of Your Truths. Halleluia.

May we thank You for daybreak, You Who first drew us to the comprehension of Your truths, Father.

04-29 "Quit you like men; be strong," Paul said, and so we pray that You would enable us to stand firmly on the Faith, Father, and follow it wherever it leads us. Lord help us each day.

"Quit you like men," Paul said, so may we stand firm for the Faith today, Father.

04-30 Kind Father, as we lift our eyes to the celestial sources of godliness, let Your Spirit inspire our thoughts and deeds, so that at the end of day we may know peace and joy.

As we lift up our eyes to the celestial Source of life, let Your spirit guide our thoughts and deeds, Father.

05-01 As we enter each new day, let us remember that success can only be attained by Your favor, Father, so help us to be deemed worthy of Your blessings. Amen and amen.

Another day we seek again to be deemed worthy of Your great blessings, Father.

05-02 May the first moments of this new day be laid on Your altar, Father. May new vistas of beauty, and new visions of service, stir us to actions that You approve and appreciate. PTL.

May new vistas and visions of service stir us to action, Father. We lay this day on Your altar.

05-03 When You have put us in the fires of affliction, You revealed Yourself as the great deliverer, as in the fiery furnace, Father. O Lord forgive, O Lord forget, our failings. Selah.

05-04 May we put on the armor of God, take up our cross, and let Your light shine wherever You have placed us in this dark world, Father of lights. Amen!

05-05 Last night we commited body and soul to Your keeping, and again, "He Who keepeth Israel neither slumbers nor sleeps." Give wisdom to those who lead church and state. PTL.

05-06 In the name of the Father and the Son, thank You for Your care through the night watches. May we appreciate our blessings and make them useful. Period.

05-07 Thy hand opens for us the gates of the morning and closes the curtains of the evening, and daily loads us wth benefits, Father. When we pitch our tent, bring us closer to home.

05-08 Thank You for blessings that abound morning and evening, Father. May we touch others in a way that leads the unredeemed soul to the Savior. Amen and AMEN!!

05-09 Thank you for the blessings that make life worth living - the love of father, mother, brother, sister, friends, and our country. May our leaders not cause us to err anymore.

05-10 Father, we assemble as a family to commune with You this morning in expectation of better days ahead for the human race in the Kingdom. Let there be an answer. Come Lord.

05-11 In early morning's light we approach Your mercy seat with awe for mercy for others, Father. We fall short, but somehow let people take notice that we have known You. Amen.

05-12 Our Father, God of the children of Israel, we have had our Egypts too, and from this wilderness we look forward to the Promised Land, the Kingdom of God on earth. Yahoo!

05-13 This morning we think of the great family of mankind, and pray for brothers and sisters the world around, Father. Bring us home tonight after fruitful toil for blissful sleep. Selah.

05-14 Father, Father, our heavenly Father, invigorated by a working man's sweet night's sleep, we give thanks and pray for another productive day today. Thank You and amen.

05-15 As the mornimg sunlight enters the window, enter and be the center of our family circle, Father and Christ, and also bless the worldwide community of believers. Let it be.

05-16 As a new day opens, may we enter its portals with a melody of praise in our hearts, Father. We pray for our home circle, but even more for that wider circle of the earth.

05-17 Thank you for the life of another day. We don't know what snares may be laid for our feet, or what trials we may have to meet, but give us the spirit of perfect trust, O Lord.

05-18 Father, show us our need of Thee, not only for salvation, but for guidance in this life. Make plain before us the pathway of duty and privilege as effective witnesses. Amen, amen!

05-19 Let us sing a new song, all the earth, and declare Your glory among the heathen, Father. Let the lives of little children, born or unborn, be more valued than gold. Halleluia!

05-20 May we say good morning and give thanks for another day's beginning, Father. Preserve us from idleness or slothfulness in matters of body or soul. Amen, selah.

05-21 Our reasons for thanksgiving are new every morning, so accept our thanks, Father. May we value our time and make good use of it, with eyes to see and hearts to understand. PTL.

05-22 We bless Thee for the privilege we have to call You Father through our Brother at Your right hand, thinking of Thy servants and prophets of old and words they passed down to us.

05-23 As we close our eyes we would open our hearts to Thee, Father. Help us work with our hands and our heads in good health for You, and have no anxious thoughts about tomorrow.

05-24 To know Thee is life, to serve You is freedom, and to pray is a privilege. May we do so without any guile or selfishness, our lives like the seamless garment of the Lord. Praise be.

05-25 We lie down in green pastures and are led to the still waters, so we pray for the restoration of our souls and for the renewal of our nation one more time. Thank You. Amen.

05-26 We come with thanksgiving in our hearts. Through another night You have kept us under the shadow of Your love, despite the poverty of our 24/7 dedication. Help us. PTL.

05-27 Beneficent Ruler of the universe, and our Father, we praise You seven times a day as David did, and ask You humbly to forgive our shortcomings, even sins of omission, selah.

05-28 We are no longer strangers and foreigners but fellow-citizens in the household of God; therefore we bend the knee - as all people will someday, thank You Abba Father. Amen

05-29 "Is not the life more than meat?," You asked. Yes we need Thee and our spiritual sustenance like the fowls of the air need their wings, Father; thus we pray. Selah.

05-30 Our privileges have been so exceedingly great, strictly by grace, that we scarce can believe it, Father, but gratefully we come to You again for Your daily blessing, PTL.

05-31 In our yesterdays we've had doors open to us as if by an angel's hand. We have been wafted on the seas of our lives safely. May You keep the wind at our backs. Halleluia.

06-01 Lord of Israel, Isaac, and Abraham, according to Your will for US, may we be willing to undertake apparently impossible missions when You indicate that it is necessary. Amen.

06-02 We look to You again, Father, so that in a new day we may get some indication as to what You would have us do, and which way You'd have us go if we have to decide. Thank You.

6-03 Thank you for life's highest privilege - access to Your throneroom in heaven - and we pray for opportunities for Your children to in some way honor Your name each day. Selah.

06-04 Thank You for a new dawn. May we come to its close unstained by conscious sin. We ask wisdom, that our choices of the day might all be right. Rebuke the wicked. Amen.

06-05 Increase our faith and use us, as You will it, as instruments for the promotion of the salvation of the world in the name of Your Son, in appreciation for Him. Let it BE!

06-06 In these latter years may we be kindly disposed toward all mankind, Father. Help the nations avoid the mistakes of the past, for the sake of the sick and the suffering. Amen!

06-07 May our hearts and hands be clean and dedicated to Your Work, Father. Keep our loved ones as under the shadow of Thy wings. Give us strength. Amen and amen.

06-08 For access to Your throneroom through the rent temple veil, through our High Priest Your son, we render thanks. Help us now as always to pray as we ought. Selah.

06-09 Admit us to Your presence, Father, and help us as we try to bring Your Good News to a sin-sick world by all means possible. Comfort the sorrowing and heal the sick.

06-10 Good morning, Lord. In these perilous times, guard us from the terror that flies by night and the arrow by mid-day. Protect our loved ones. Thy Kingdom come, Lord.

06-11 By Thy goodness we have encountered the duties of another day, so may we this day show forth Thy praise with our lips and our lives. In His name, amen and amen.

06-12 We come to the throne of grace as You have bidden us, Father, notwithstanding our shortcomings, that we may be a blessing to others and find a place in Your Kingdom.

06-13 Today may we make our Master discernable to someone who has not yet beheld Him, Father. Thank You for Your infinite solicitude. Make wars to cease. AMEN.

06-14 May we find medicine for the mind and food for the soul in your Scriptures, Father. Bless this planet with an outpouring of Your holy spirit upon all flesh. Let it be!

06-15 Father, what a privilege it is to come into Your presence directly every morning, noon, and night! May we somehow be a blessing to someone who needs help today. Amen.

06-16 We awake to the joy of one more morning, thanks to You our everliving Father. Give us the ready word of cheer for anyone who may cross our path today. Selah.

06-17 Our everloving Father, for having called us into Your Family, we ask that You would accept our thanksgiving. Grant us the prosperity of a rich and secure Faith. Halleluia.

06-18 Thank You for refreshing sleep, and for the privileges of a new day, Father. Abide with us all day and make us strong to do Your will and help us to be a part of Your Work. Amen.

06-19 Heavenly Father, we lift up our hearts gratefully to Thee this new day. Guide us by Thy spirit in the way most pleasing to Thee today. Let Your names be praised 7 times a day.

06-20 May the very spirit of Your Son now cry "ABBA," and may we love and serve our fellows as potential members of that great happy family of God on earth, and forever. Selah.

06-21 Father, may we true our conscience daily and act accordingly. Deliver us from worldly "wisdom." Stay the madness of men who teach envy, strife, and division. Amen.

06-22 May we be enabled to see more clearly Your goodness and our privileges as Sons of God, Father. Enable us to also understand our obligations and requirements. Hallelu !!

06-23 As privileges again arise to meet us, we pause to pray for Your worldwide family of potential children, especially for those who witness for You in hard places. Glory be!

06-24 Speaking of privileges, thank You for the open door to Your throne room in the third heaven, Father. So overrule that peace can be maintained among all nations. Amen.

06-25 Our unchanging Lord, as we recall many revelations of Your assistance, many of the desires of our hearts granted, on this morning allow us to express our gratefulness. Selah.

06-26 O Lord our Lord, how excellent are Your names. Accept our thanksgiving and pour out upon all people

Your holy spirit and give hope to those without hope. Halleluliah.

06-27 May this new day open up new opportunities of service, Father. We seek direction along right ways that will not dim our vision of the ideal, or Your final triumph. Amen.

06-28 May we give thanks that You sanctified marriage and the family and, as children of the heavenly Father, we ask that all nations may be brought into One Family. Halleluia !!

06-29 Almighty Shepherd of our souls, we approach Your unveiled mercy seat in the name of Your only begotten Son. May Your benediction apply to this family circle. Praise the Lord.

06-30 Father, Father, create in us a clean heart and a right spirit, that the words of our mouths and the meditations of our hearts may be acceptable in Your sight, O Lord and Redeemer!

07-01 Father, spare us from spiritual aristocracy, for even the best of Thy children see as through a dark glass. Let us not use fear nor sneer, but let us just help others. Amen!

07-02 We are in the valley of dark shadows, but we see Your glory when we lift up our eyes to the hilltops, Father. Fill our hearts with hopeand make us a blessing to others. Thank You.

07-03 As we have been spared to see the morning light, accept our thanksgiving for this and countless other blessings, but we need special mercy for our nation, Father. Selah.

07-04 Bless our nation. May it hold high the standard of godliness, and fly the flag of Freedom for as long as You can extend our shaky lease on life, Father. Amen.

07-05 We turn to the light of the morning and thank You for the night's rest, Father. May Thy church be a light to the nation, and the nation a light to all nations. May it yet be done.

07-06 "Do you believe me NOW?," Christ asked. As we enter the duties of a new day, we believe, and we need Him to share our yoke for the accomplishment of our mission. PTL.

07-07 Daily Thou dost load us with benefits, but let us not be indifferent to Thy goodness, Father. Let us live our praise and be a benefit to our neighbors around the world. Amen!

07-08 Today we pray that every member of this household may be assured that You have a purpose for every human. May that be the highest ambition for each and every day. Selah.

07-09 Bless our homes and the homeless, and our hands in helping one another, Father, and at last may we find a home in Your heavenly Kingdom on earth for 1,000 years. Amen.

07-10 Feed us with the bread of heaven, Father, and may it so fill our hearts with Your spirit that others will take note that we have been with Thee today and always. "Let it be."

07-11 We unite as a family, Father, to give praise and invoke upon our home Thy gracious heavenly blessing. Defend us from the seductive snares of secularism always. Selah.

07-12 Thank You Father for the tokens of Your presence in the beauty of sunrise and sunset, the song of birds, the fragrance of flowers, and the laughter of children. Halleluiah, amen!

07-13 Good morning, Father. We are persuaded that neither death, nor principalities, nor powers, nor things to come shall be able to separate us from Your love. Amen.

07-14 We must say You have preserved us day by day until this morning hour, Father, and in spite of our failings, we continue to pray. Make us fervent in spirit and in business. Amen.

07-15 "Give thy strength unto Thy servant and save the son of Thine handmaid," David said. I pray "Save Your servants, yes, but also save all the children of Your people in the USA. Selah.

07-16 May Thy Good spirit make Thee so real to us today that when its hours have passed away forever, there will be no memory of failure, Father. Selah, amen, let it be.

07-17 ABBA FATHER, may Your spirit enable us to fight a bold fight for the right, and let the close of this day find us still on the narrow path to the Kingdom of God. So be it.

07-18 Today as ever we thank You for the revelation of Thy love in the arms of affection to which our baby hearts responded, Father. Thank You for mothers who taught us to pray, PTL.

07-19 Help us today not to disappoint You in Your desires for us, Father. Dwell in us and work through us until we become indeed lights to the world. Have mercy on all peoples, please.

07-20 In the morning I will direct my prayer unto Thee, and look up! To know that the great Creator is our Father is to have all prayers heard before they are asked. Amen and selah.

07-21 For the blessings of a new day we desire to thank You and ask Your direction, Father, until finally we come to our Father's home and unbroken family circles, praise the Lord.

07-22 This day purge our ears of worldly noises until they are quick to receive heavenly songs. Lead all true seekers to some spiritual Bethlehem, and rulers to the right cause. Selah.

07-23 Thank You for the blessing of another day, and the chance to grow in grace, Father. Help us and hear us as we pray for suffering humanity, and grant us world peace. Amen.

07-24 As the sun rises again, we see new proofs of Your favor, Father. And when our race will have been run, forgive us and receive us into Thine everlasting habitations. Halleluiah.

07-25 As we welcome a new day, we beseech Thee for the diligence and the energy for the discharge of the duties of our calling, Father. May we be fervent in spirit always. Selah.

07-26 May we find delight in work today and choose that task that most taxes our highest powers, and best serves the world's needs, Father. Let us do it fervently. Praise God.

07-27 Thank You for forgiving our lack of filial affection from earliest childhood, Father. May we trust Your Providence completely even when we cannot trace the reasons. Thank You!

07-28 May we have complete trust that You will direct us and bring to pass that which is for our good, Father. Help Your witnesses help more people to seek and find You. Selah.

07-29 Grant us a clearer vision of our field of service, and may our fellowship with Thee be unbroken today. May the day come soon when all the earth shall seek refuge in Thee. Amen.

07-30 May we give in running-over measures, so that those who receive may become generous too. May we and they be happy to correct our ways, Father. Praise Your names.

07-31 "WHOSOEVER will may come and drink of the water of Life freely." So, freely we have received and freely we give. Help us to overcome the evil in our nature, Father. Amen.

08-01 May this gift of a new day be a day for serving You, as Your heirs and not as aliens, and when the twilight falls, Father, may we sleep in peace under the shadow of Your wings.

08-02 Given another day to seek the ideal, help us to move forward and grow, aware of Your past favors, and to love the Truth and to eshew evil more and more. Selah.

08-03 May we come before Your mercy seat to loosen and lose our burdens, Father, and we ask it in that Name by which all Your precious promises will surely be fulfilled.

08-04 May we interpret our blessings in terms of obligations as well as privilege, Father. As you have made us rich in blessings and peace, make us also rich in gratitude. Selah.

08-05 May we be guarded today from ungodly enticements Father. Give us rather the vision of the upward pathway of our calling, and Your personal omnipotent presence. Selah.

08-06 May the Truth be passed on, as it came down to us, that Thou art the alpha and the omega, the Promise and Fulfillment, Father. Help us to make this new day count. Selah.

08-07 You know our frame Father, as a father who pities his children, so in this new day, set Your angels about us and guide us 'til twilight falls, and we sleep in peace again. Amen.

08-08 Another day to live: let us make our home like the one in Bethany, where the Lord loved to go. And make our schools places children love to go again! Let us praise His name.

08-09 Father, we but dimly comprehend and but partly understand You and Your thoughts - Paul said we see through dark glasses - but help us to *grow* in understanding. Selah.

08-10 "You have compassed this mountain long enough; go ye north," You told our forebears. If we are at anther turning point, guide Your people, spiritual Israel, again. Amen.

08-11 May He lift up His countenance upon us, and give you peace. Halleluliah. Such a deal!

08-12 May we be begotten with with a new awareness of our weaknesses and our spiritual needs, Father, and help us to walk courageously in the faith of our fathers. Selah.

08-13 May we not presume upon Your providence; forgive our lack of filial affection, Father, and as we recall the past, make us stronger for the future we face. Selah.

08-14 In the morning You have given us another day, every minute of which can be put to prayer, meditation, study, and serving You. Make every hour count, Father. Amen.

08-15 May we walk in the footsteps of the healing, redeeming, Shepherd of the sheepfold, so that our wills may be conformed to Yours. May Your commands be our pleasure.

08-16 May we catch a clearer vision of what we can do for our people, and even as a mustard seed cannot germinate without water, let us soak in living water from Above. Selah.

08-17 May we influence positively those who can change, have the sense to avoid those who cannot, Father. Help us, and keep us from those who mean us harm. Halleluiah.

08-18 Lord we believe, but help our unbelief if that is ever an issue, because we want the world to know You as a Father as well as the Supreme Judge of the universe. Say amen.

08-19 Oh help us each day, the bitterest as well as the brightest, to have such a vibrant sense of Your presence that we may act according to Your ineffable love for us. Praise Your names.

08-20 For the dawn of another day we give thanks. We commend to Your care friends and family members who are getting older. Bless the church they once remembered. Selah!

08-21 May we be as consecrated as Samuel and John the Baptist in our own way and times, Father. Bless those in authority in this world with wisdom and compassion. Amen.

08-22 In distress I called upon You, Father, and you rescued me. Help us to encourage those who need courage, wisdom to the foolish. Praise the Lord. Amen.

08-23 May we acknowledge Thee in all our days, that You may direct our paths, Father, and let our relationships be consecrated by the touch of Your hand, Lord. Hallelu!

08-24 Father, Father, our heavenly Father, thank you for Your watchcare over us during the night, and we pray no less for the day, and for all people everywhere. Selah.

08-25 May thy Way to peace be made known, and Thy saving health among all nations, Father. New to us are Thy mercies in the morning, and sweet in the evening.

08-26 Sobered by the days that have been, may we be strong enough for the day that is ahead of us, Father. May we be helpful to our fellow pilgrims along life's way. Selah.

08-27 "Blessed are the pure in heart," and may our very lives be pure so that all things might be pure to us, Father. And bless the peacemakers, our police officers and others.

08-28 As this day is, so may our strength be, Father. May we dwell in the secret place of the Most High and be allowed at last a place in Your family's Kingdom. The Lord be praised.

08-29 Make this a good day to go to work, and may we be among those who hunger and thirst after the godliness that produces blessings and joy and peace, Father. Selah.

08-30 "We thank Thee for the night, and the pleasant morning light," Father, and we seek the grace to overcome evil with good. Let the wicked keep silence. Let it be. Halleluiah, amen.

08-31 As morning breaks gently upon us, we would draw inspiration and instruction from high and holy things. By our serving bring someone into Your sheepfold. Selah.

09-01 May we greet another day with Your guardian angels continuing to watch over us, and at day's end, may we know that we are one day closer to Home, Father. Amen and amen.

09-02 Behold, we are the sons of God, to whom we are indebted for another day's work. Father, as sons and daughters we just commit everything unto you. Halleluiah, amen.

09-03 May we today come to You with more earnestness of desire than we sometimes have comek Father. Deliver us from over-estimating the value of today's transitory things. Selah.

09-04 May we, reaching a new day's threshold, be guided into wider fields of usefulness, new regions of service, aware of the world's desperate need of the Good News.

09-05 We bring nothing in our folded hands to buy blessings, Father, but help us to bring blessings to others. Help us to stand in the gap and make up the hedge for them. Selah.

09-06 May we redeem the time, purchase our opportunities, and make our blessings count, Father. And make us effective channels of blessings into a lost, deceived, sick world.

09-07 May we, even like plants that turn toward the sun, seek your light in a dark world, Father. We think of those who are in spiritual dungeons, that they may find Your Light.

09-08 May we be conscious in some measure of our shortcomings by nature and seek Your grace. To each member of this family circle grant such blessings as are especially needed.

09-09 We "come boldly unto the Throne of Grace" for faith, Father. Help us to "hold fast our profession," not our possessions. Order our pathway of life. Amen.

09-10 Today and always, may we be cheerful, self-forgetful, temperate, and pure of speech, Father, and may others be drawn to You and Your ways, in Your Son's name, amen.

09-11 May you breathe into us Your spirit, shine through our eyes, and throb with our hearts, Father. Bring this world back from the brink, lest we leave behind just an empty dish.

09-12 May we walk humbly with You, but we come boldly before You, asking that we can stand firm and perform every duty that devolves upon us today, Father. Selah.

09-13 May You employ our lives one more day in Your service Father. Make us a blessing to others, and may at least one lost soul be saved today, in His name. Verily, selah.

09-14 May we gather and give thanks for the night's respite from care, Father. We await Your instruction for us today as Your stewards, that our time and talents may be put to use.

09-15 O Thou Who hast sanctified marriage and established the home, bless this our home with Your presence. May the children hold dear the lessons they learn here. Selah.

09-16 May our thanks be accepted this morning, thanks for Your presence in our lives, and for the availability of transformation for any who desire to change and to grow in grace.

09-17 Designer and Creator, protect us as we live in a sinful world. Let us show our praise, Father. Give a double portion of Your spirit to Your pastors and witnesses. Selah.

09-18 Save us from ungodly desires and carnal impulsess of our own thoughts, Father. Let Your face shine in our faces, and the Taskmaster's work in our work today. PTL.

09-19 Though people are discouraged, but may we all look up and see an army of angels coming someday, like the servant of the prophet Elisha. Open our eyes and our ears.

09-20 May no corrupt communication proceed from our mouths, or even the silent thought, so that You may eventually speak with our tongues and work with our hands. Selah.

09-21 In this world, tolerance may reach such a level that intelligent people will be banned from speaking so as not to offend imbeciles, but help us speak the Truth anyway, Father.

09-22 May the Word of salvation be preached and not returned unto Thee void, Father, and comfort anyone in pain or grief or trouble "as one whose mother comforteth." Selah.

09-23 May we have wherewith to respond to those who reproach us, Father, and if any inquire as to the reason for the Hope that resides within us, give us the words. Selah.

09-24 May we be prepared for all the appointments of Your coming Kingdom, Father. Help us to be overcomers and endure to the end of our appointed days in this life. Selah.

09-25 May Your perfect plans and purposes be fulfilled, especially for Your special witnesses, Father, and give them souls pulled from the fire like Shadrac, Meshek, and Abednigo.

09-26 "Having shut thy door, pray," You said, Father, so in the quiet time of a new day let us so pray and so listen as to discern Your still small voice after society's storms. Selah.

09-27 May our homes be a *home* in every sense of the word, where parents and children know what is right, where Your spirit both reigns and rains from above, Father.

09-28 For the privilege of prayer, meditation, and study we praise Thee. Help us to use these tools so our lives as well as our lips can tell of our great gratitude, Father. Selah.

09-29 May the Son of man and the Son of God arise with healing in His wings, for the nations of the earth, for every tribe and every tongue, sooner rather than later, Father.

09-30 As we prepare to turn another page on the calender, let the lessons of the last month give us all the wisdom and foresight that we can handle, as we seek Thy will, Father. Selah.

10-01 May we find joy in our toil, triumph in our trials, and understanding in our thinking, with Thy still small voice and the holy spirit as our guide, Father. Selah.

10-02 Praise the Lord seven times a day! We have lived to live another day, so may Your sustaining grace enable us to accomplish the work You have given us to do.

10-03 The Lord's is our glory. No gift or any good thing will You withhold from those who walk uprightly. Thank You for the blessings of the day that is gone, and for today's. Selah.

10-04 May the morning's alarm be our call to prayer, Father. Thank You for every good and perfect gift, including evidences of Your protection from harm to us and ours.

10-05 As with all our days, help us this day to avoid living for this world alone or this life only. Let us so live and give that others may see You in us. Praise all of Your holy names. Selah.

10-06 Happy is the nation that has the God of Jacob for its help, whose hope is in the Lord of Hosts, and that holds Your Law in high esteem. Woe unto the wicked. Amen.

10-07 May this gift of a new day be a day of preparation for that great new day for all mankind when You will pour out Your spirit upon all flesh, Father. Selah.

10-08 Now rested and refreshed, we appeal to You in the spirit of consecration for an enhanced sensitivity to Your presence and Your purposes and plans for us, Father.

10-09 May we walk humbly with You today with the help of the power of Your spirit, and by its power help us to be fishers of men. So guide us in that endeavor, Father. Selah.

10-10 If darkness, doubts, or discouragement should ever come over us Father, may we experience the blessed assurance of blissful redemption, guidance, and love, Father.

10-11 May we all come to the end of this day all the wiser because of it, Lord. May all peoples and their rulers wake up to their *need* to be under Your sovereign rule. Shalom.

10-12 As day dawns, let us seek first the things we need *most*, and help us to serve neighbors in need, Father. Please stay the madness of those who talk and teach strife. Shalom.

10-13 May we begin the life of the new day grateful for it, Father, and let not trifles ruffle our tempers, but give us words fitly spoken and sunshiny faces all the day. Halleluliah.

10-14 The Apostle Paul said "Pray without ceasing," so let us begin in the early morning quiet hours. Let Your Son so live in us so that others might see Him in us. Amen, amen.

10-15 At the dawning of another day, may we perceive more evidences of Your favor, Father, and may we manifest the spirit of the Messiah in all we think, say, and do. Selah.

10-16 May we thank You this morning for life, for friends and family, and for surviving to see another day, Elohim. May we follow in Your footsteps as Your Son's spiritual brethren.

10-17 May we have an attitude of gratitude today, Abba Father, and help us to help You make this world a little better place for our having lived this day. For Your sake, Selah and shalom.

10-18 May there be comfort for the sorrowful and peace for the grieving the world over, Father, and may we be useful clay in the hands of the Great Potter. Hallelulliah.

10-19 May we, when that great homecoming happens, be found among that great multitude that no man can number, Father. Forgive us wherein we may have fallen short. Selah.

10-20 Father, we but dimly comprehend the complexities of the physical universe, and only partly perceive the Spiritual one, but we know that we need Thee every hour. Shalom.

10-21 May we not add to the sum of this world's evils, but rather set ourselves one more day firmly against them, Father, for the sake of Your Kingdom's coming as soon as possible. Selah.

10-22 May we have eyes to see, and open hearts to receive, the Truth, and thank you in advance. May many of the lost, by way of the cross, be redeemed this year. Selah.

10-23 Father, Your innumerable blessings are fresh every morning and new every evening, so we commend ourselves into Your everlasting arms. Help us make our blessings count.

10-24 May we not consider ourselves too good to mingle with the lowly, Father. Forgive any shortcomings, so that at evening there may be no sad friction between memory and remorse.

10-25 May we with a new day of privileges present ourselves as living sacrifices for whatever servces that Your gifts may require of us, lest we ignore Your claims upon us, Father. Selah.

10-26 On the cusp of a new day, may we go forth to battle and defeat spiritual darkness, Father. We love this land, so give it a new transfusion of Your spirit's healing power.

10-27 May we give thanks for the care lavished on us in our early days, the love of two parents, and the patience of teachers. May we use the love with which we have been dowered to panoply ourselves against the wicked foe and all evil, Father.

10-28 May we give thanks for the tasks we have been given, and may we do them with all our might. Help us,

Father, if we are ever tempted to put the temporary things above the eternal.

10-29 May we come, some with heavy hearts, but with thankful hearts, before Your throne, Father, knowing that at the end of this life we can live again with You forever. Selah.

10-30 May we be glad to see the dawning of another day, Father. Since You said "If you ask anything in My Name, I will do it," we ask that more and more people wake up.

10-31 May we as believers, have the wisdom to understand Your will - and the grace to obey it - among ourselves and among all with whom we have to do. Fit us for our tasks. Selah.

11-01 May we not just believe in You but literally *believe* You, Father. In spite of our short fallings, we look forward to meeting You in person, our real Father!

11-02 May we, like little children, come to You to pray: Let all who belong to us belong to you, and hasten the day when You will reign in every heart, hearth, and home. Selah.

11-03 May we remember that kind words never die, and like the great Burden Bearer, may we tactfully enter into the needs and burdens of others, with Your help, Father.

11-04 May we have some part in Your Work, and some place in Your service, Lord, like branches on the vine, and may laborers be sent out into the fields ripe to the harvest.

11-05 May our faces be set toward Thee as we set out upon another day, Father. If loneliness be anyone's lot, let them discover Your never-sleeping companionship and care. Selah.

11-06 May we come to You as children come to an earthly parent, Father. We laid us down in peace and have awakened with renewed purpose; help those who know no peace.

11-07 May we find enjoyment in the work which in Your Providence has been assigned to us, Father, and thank You also for the privilege of giving others a rising hope. Selah.

11-08 May the light of Your truths shine into us and through us into a dark world, Father. Let Your spirit descend from on high upon all peoples as soon as possible we pray, please.

11-09 May we be appreciative of a child's right of approach and the gift of expectancy, Father. Let Your will be our unmasked passion and Your service our pleasure every day. Selah.

11-10 May we give thanks that we have ived to live another day, Father, and prepare us for all that You are preparing for us and the whole wide world. Let it be. Selah.

11-11 [Veterans Day] May we true in the midst of all that is false, clean in the midst of godlessness, and clear in our witnessing, Father, and find true peace at our firesides.

11-12 May we seek the Kingdom first, Father, instead of mere money, power, or prestige. We only ask for the peace that surpasses human understanding, and for wisdom. Selah.

11-13 May we, as brothers of the race, become more like the Messiah, working upwards on the slopes of service, Father. Make this a super day for the human race. Amen.

11-14 May we, in the spirit of the faith of our fathers, have grateful hearts and go ever onward in the footsteps of our Elder Brother and our Lord. Praise be unto Him. Selah.

11-15 Thank You for the privilege of duties in a new day, Father, and may we experience Your daily redemption, guidance, sustenance, and inspiration - as in "Your spirit IN US."

11-16 May we, rested and refreshed, so walk and so work today that at day's end we can say that we have furthered Your Work and brought the Kingdom perhaps one day closer.

11-17 May our lamplights so shine today - in the home, in the streets, and in the workplace - that You may be able to draw people to Yourself Father. Comfort the comfortless.

11-18 May we come with grateful hearts before Your throne of grace, Father, to boldly seek Your Kingdom and Your godliness first. Help us to demonstrate our gratitude. Amen.

11-19 May we not become preoccupied with worldly affairs, but we do pray for those who fight against You, against each other, and against themselves, Father. Shalom.

11-20 May we not come as aliens or strangers but as Your own true children of light, Father, that our witness may have an evangel in the influence we exert day by day. Selah.

11-21 May we become the salt of the earth, with as great a zeal as our fathers had, to help make America a shining city set on a hll that cannot be hid, Father, for Your Son's sake.

11-22 May it be in our hearts to be grateful for the privilege of serving You every day of our lives as Your sons and daughters, Father, and help us this day to put on Your spiritual armor.

11-23 May we come to the Throne, not as orphans or strangers, but as heirs through our Elder Brother, helping to prepare the way for His Second Coming, Father. Halleluiah!

11-24 May we be prepared to accept any mission upon which You choose to send us, Father. Deliver us from the fear of man, and temper the storms for your shorn lambs. Selah.

11-25 Thank You, thank You, for life, limb, and Liberty, heavenly Father. "Unto whom much hath been given, much is required," so thank You for the privilege of duty. Amen.

11-26 May we remember that the great questions are the issues of eternity. Guide, Great God, in the affairs of state. Bless godly citizen groups, and give us Your benediction. Selah.

11-27 May your angels be set beside us to keep us from falling, beneath us to lift us out of the filth, behind us to give us a shove in the right direction, above us to quench the fiery darts of the devil, and before us to show us the way home.

11-28 We thank You for your presence in our hearts and homes, and for get-togethers with brethren and kin, heavenly Father. May You be with us 'til we all meet again. PTL!

11-29 Father, breathe into us the spirit of teachableness and godliness again today. Send forth laborers into the harvest to teach the way of peace and happiness. Halleluiah.

11-30 For the rest of the night under the shadow of Your wings, we thank You. We pray that likewise You would protect our children and oversee our institutions of learning.

12-01 As we go forth to our individual duties, give us the zeal and enthusiasm and that wisdom that comes down from above, which is easily to be entreated and peaceable. Selah.

12-02 Thank You for the rest and refreshment of the night and the sight of another day dawning. Help us to accomplish something good today, heavenly Father. Amen.

12-03 We thank Thee Christ for our access to the throne in the third heaven. You and the Father work; let us so work too that we may be worthy of Your rewards. Thank You, amen.

12-04 For a new day's dawn we bless Thee, Elohim Addonai. May we to some extent be worthy of its arrival, and do things worthwhile for the church and the human race today.

12-05 Henceforth there is laid up for us a crown of righteousness; let no man take our crown, nor let us throw it all away someday, Giver of every good and perfect gift, thank You. Selah.

12-06 Father we bring our home and our hearts to Thee this morning for the blessing You have intended for us. Having You we have all, so let us go and share. Hallelu, amen.

12-07 This race, the *human* race, has had its "last chance," MacArthur said, and the solution must be "of the spirit." Pour out Your spirit upon all flesh, Father, before it's too late.

12-08 Father, give us a due sense of all Thy blessings, and help us to focus on whatsoever things are lovely, pure, praiseworthy, virtuous, just, of good repute, and TRUE.

12-09 O Lord our God, bountiful benefactor of the families of the earth, help the homeless, comfort the grieving, bring Your Kingdom as soon as possible, and accept our gratitude.

12-10 "Six days shall we labor," but for freedom of conscience we pause one day to assemble. Preserve our precious Liberties, Father, and help us to make good use of them.

12-11 Inhabitor of the heavens, there is no way by which to reach out to Thee except One Way - the Truth, our Redeemer and elder Brother. We thank You for Him at day's dawn.

12-12 Thank You for Thy Word the Bible. Help us to appreciate it, understand it, and obey it, Father. Save our country and bless Your ecclesia, Your whole Church, as You know it. Amen.

12-13 Our Father, You are the center and the circumference of our lives, our Morning Star, our Lily of the Valley. Speak to our hearts by all means possible. Hush the clamor. Be praised.

12-14 As children of the morning, we go to a quiet place to commune, to listen for Your voice after the storms, Father. Have pity on the sufferings of the sons of men. Come soon.

12-15 May we this day give the world far more in spiritual blessings than we get in material things. Let the Gospel of the preparation of peace be proclaimed to the whole planet asap.

12-16 As the dawn has dawned, we thank You for the Hope of Glory and evidence of things not seen, and when the dusk falls, give light for the way home, and abide with us, Father.

12-17 Father, purge our minds of all unreality and the dross of inappropriate desires. Revive our first love and quicken it into a blazing flame. Let us pray without ceasing. Amen.

12-18 For the work of the new may we have strength; from the storms of life may we be protected like the chicks by the hen, Father, and save us in the hollow of Your hand.

12-19 We thank You for the fact that You have so revealed Yourself to us that we know that You are our heavenly Father. Help us to use this day for Your Kingdom's glory. Amen.

12-20 You have opened Your hand and supplied all our needs and then some. Thank You, our Father and our Brother. Let all the nations now worship in spirit and in Truth and sing "amen"!

12-21 Our heavenly Father, You have allowed us to get to this day by both miraculous and mundane means. We celebrate Your mercy, Your mighty works, and miracles yet to come.

12-22 Father, You have never failed us though we have fallen short of even our own ideals and values. We just ask that You can accept our petitions and use us as You know best. Selah.

12-23 "As the mountains surrounding Jerusalem," and as Moses upon Mt. Sinai, we look unto the hills, from whence cometh our help, God of Abraham, Isaac, and Jacob. Halelluiah.

12-24 Around our family altar Lord, we come and seek Your face. Have mercy on the human race and make us fruitful by Your Grace, Father. Amen.

12-25 We give thanks that our Redeemer was begotten by Your power, whatever time of year it was, Father, and thank You for the angels and prophets who foretold that. Sing Halelluiah!

12-26 Our Father, whose glory fills the universes, make us conscious this morning that You are not far off or are unaware of our needs down here. Send our Savior as soon as possible.

12-27 O Lord, who seeeth everything, help us take up our crosses and follow Thee. We turn the world's suffering over to Thee, for You work in marvelous ways Your wonders to perform.

12-28 Thank You, thank You that the grave was robbed of its Victim after three days and three nights. May we live our lives as those who will be raised up with Him. Amen.

12-29 If we should ever have a winter of despair, save us, Father. We pray that our flight be not in the winter, nor on the Sabbath day. Help us to be worthy.

12-30 Ere we venture into whatever this new day holds for us, Father, touch us with that hand which was laid in blessing upon those who went before us. Amen.

12-31 Upon the cusp of a new day and the threshold of a new year, we look up unto You, Father. May the chalice of the world's wine not bring bitterness tomorrow.

/_____

Your mission, should you choose to accept it, is to use this book every day without fail.

Printed in the United States
by Baker & Taylor Publisher Services